OIL FIELD WORKER

BY CHRIS BOWMAN

TORQUE™

BELLWETHER MEDIA · MINNEAPOLIS, MN

TM

Are you ready to take it to the extreme?
Torque books thrust you into the action-packed world
of sports, vehicles, mystery, and adventure. These books
may include dirt, smoke, fire, and dangerous stunts.
WARNING: read at your own risk.

Library of Congress Cataloging-in-Publication Data

Bowman, Chris, 1990- author.
  Oil Field Worker / By Chris Bowman.
    pages cm. -- (Torque: Dangerous Jobs)
  Summary: "Engaging images accompany information about oil field workers. The combination of
high-interest subject matter and light text is intended for students in grades 3 through 7"-- Provided
by publisher.
  Audience: Ages 7-12.
  Audience: Grades 3 to 7.
  Includes bibliographical references and index.
  ISBN 978-1-62617-111-4 (hardcover : alk. paper)
  1. Oil well drilling--Juvenile literature. 2. Oil fields--Accidents--Juvenile literature. 3. Petroleum industry
and trade--Employees--Juvenile literature. I. Title. II. Series: Dangerous jobs (Minneapolis, Minn.)
  TN871.2.B636 2014
  622.3382'023--dc23
                                        2013051211

This edition first published in 2015 by Bellwether Media, Inc.

Printed in the United States of America, North Mankato, MN.

TABLE OF CONTENTS

EXPLOSION!

An oil field worker is in the middle of his shift on an **oil rig**. He checks the pressure in the pipes. The pressure is high. Something must be stuck in the pipes! The worker races to lower the pressure before it is too late.

He opens the pipes to let more oil through. But he is too late. The pipe explodes. He is thrown many feet from the rig! Other workers rush to save him. Soon an ambulance arrives. The oil field worker lives. He is one of the lucky few to survive an oil field accident.

CHAPTER 2

OIL FIELD WORKERS

Oil field workers manage drilling rigs called **derricks**. These workers are often called **roughnecks**. They drill deep into the ground in search of oil. Then they ready the machines that remove oil from the ground.

derrick

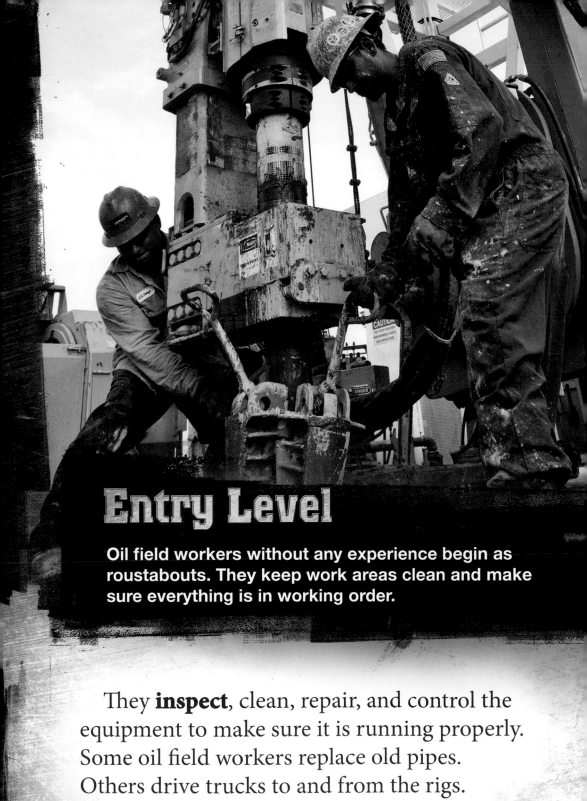

Entry Level

Oil field workers without any experience begin as roustabouts. They keep work areas clean and make sure everything is in working order.

They **inspect**, clean, repair, and control the equipment to make sure it is running properly. Some oil field workers replace old pipes. Others drive trucks to and from the rigs.

Oil field workers come from many different backgrounds. Many have some experience working with heavy equipment or in construction. Some workers have studied metalworking or **mechanics** in school. Most are trained on the job. They learn **first aid** and other important skills.

Boom and Bust

Many people compare working on the oil fields to the gold rush of the 1800s. When oil is found, workers pour into the area. This creates a booming city. When the oil is gone, workers move on to the next field. They leave trails of empty towns behind.

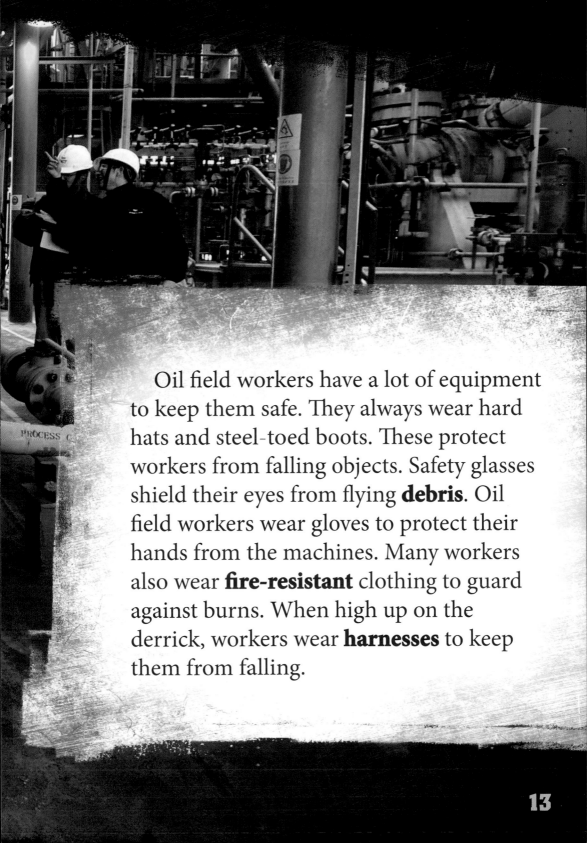

Oil field workers have a lot of equipment to keep them safe. They always wear hard hats and steel-toed boots. These protect workers from falling objects. Safety glasses shield their eyes from flying **debris**. Oil field workers wear gloves to protect their hands from the machines. Many workers also wear **fire-resistant** clothing to guard against burns. When high up on the derrick, workers wear **harnesses** to keep them from falling.

CHAPTER 3
DANGER!

Oil field workers face many dangers on the rig. Lifting heavy objects can cause injuries. Sometimes drilling releases **toxic fumes** from the ground. These can cause workers to get sick or even die. Workers also risk falling from ladders and **catwalks** high on rig **masts**.

High Up

Most roughnecks work on the floor of the rig. This is often 30 feet (9 meters) above the ground!

Because the oil business is booming, many old rigs are being brought back into use. Most lack new safety features. Rigs have many spinning chains and cables. Workers risk injury or death from getting caught in or hit by these.

Roughnecks can get crushed if a heavy rig **collapses**. Too much pressure in pipes can cause an explosion. Fires or flying pieces from these can harm workers. Drilling for oil is also very loud. It can be hard to communicate dangers to others.

Parts of an Oil Rig

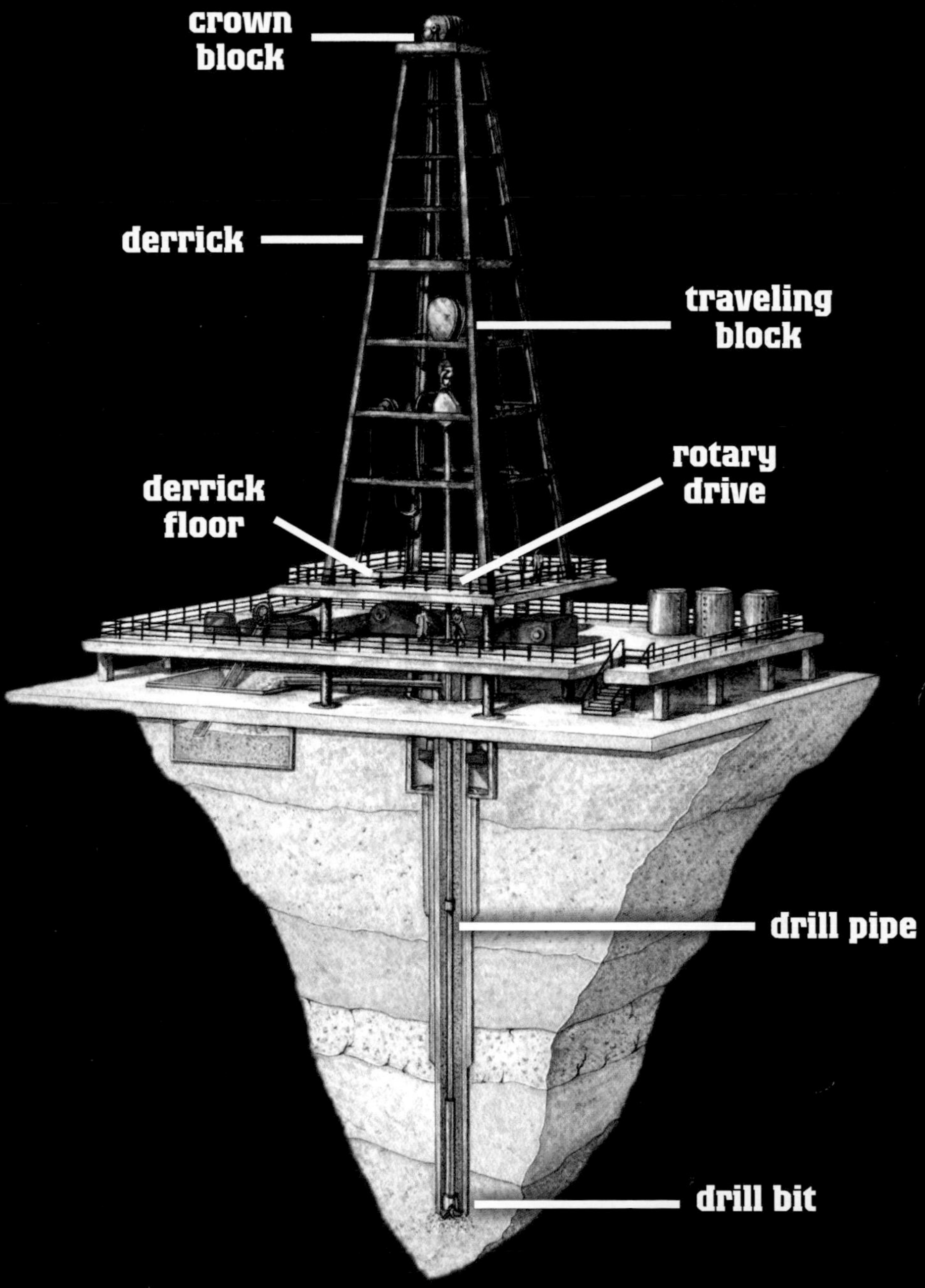

crown block

derrick

traveling block

rotary drive

derrick floor

drill pipe

drill bit

Most rigs never stop drilling. Roughnecks must work through storms and extreme weather. In the summer, workers can get overheated. In the winter, workers risk **frostbite** and **hypothermia**. Oil field workers often work 12-hour shifts for a week straight before they get time off. Tired people are more likely to make mistakes. This puts them more at risk for accidents on the rig.

Oil field workers are well aware of the risks of their job. They could be hurt or killed in many different ways. But the risk is worth it to them. They like the money and the excitement of their fast-paced job.

Tragedy on the Job

On November 5, 2013, Alexis Anderson was working as a pumper on an oil rig near McLeansboro, Illinois. His clothing got caught in the pumping equipment. He was crushed when the moving parts pulled him into the machine.

Glossary

catwalks—narrow, elevated walkways on oil rigs

collapses—falls suddenly

debris—the remains of something that has been destroyed

derricks—the structures over oil wells that support the drilling machinery

fire-resistant—difficult to burn

first aid—emergency medical care given to a sick or injured person before he or she reaches a hospital

frostbite—a condition in which the body tissues are damaged by extreme cold

harnesses—straps that attach someone to a rope or line

hypothermia—a condition in which the body loses heat faster than it can produce it; hypothermia causes body systems to shut down.

inspect—to carefully examine; oil field workers inspect rigs to make sure they are safe.

masts—vertical towers on oil rigs

mechanics—the study of the design, construction, and operation of machines or tools

oil rig—a structure that holds equipment to drill for oil

roughnecks—workers on an oil rig; roughneck is a specific position but is often used to refer to any oil rig worker that is not a driller.

toxic fumes—gases that are poisonous to living beings

To Learn More

AT THE LIBRARY

Horn, Geoffrey M. *Oil Rig Roughneck.* Pleasantville, N.Y.:
Gareth Stevens Pub., 2008.

Nelson, Drew. *Life on an Oil Rig.* New York, N.Y.: Gareth
Stevens Publishing, 2013.

Thomas, William David. *Oil Rig Worker.* New York, N.Y.:
Marshall Cavendish Benchmark, 2011.

ON THE WEB

Learning more about oil field workers
is as easy as 1, 2, 3.

1. Go to www.factsurfer.com.

2. Enter "oil field workers" into the search box.

3. Click the "Surf" button and you will see a list of
related web sites.

With factsurfer.com, finding more information
is just a click away.

Index